TOWNS IN GERMANY
P O T S D A M

POTSDAM

Photographs   MANFRED HAMM

Introduction   HANS-JOACHIM GIERSBERG

NICOLAI

©1991 Nicolaische Verlagsbuchhandlung
Beuermann GmbH
Translation: Ann Robertson

Historical Illustrations: Staatliche Schlösser
und Gärten Potsdam-Sanssouci

POTSDAM

On 4. August 1751, the Italian Count Francesco Algarotti (1712–1764), a friend and councellor on art matters to Frederick the Great, wrote in a letter to the King: "Potsdam will become a school of architecture, just as it is a school in the art of war." Admittedly, these lines referred merely to a general trend in architectural design at the time, yet both aspects were central to the former and future development of Potsdam which had been a royal residential town since the middle of the 17. century. In Algarotti's day, the town itself was already over five hundred years old.

A first reference was made in a document dating 993 to "Poztupimi" where a settlement had emerged near the castle which protected a crossing point on the Havel. The town was awarded civic status in 1317 but for hundreds of years it hardly developed as it lay in marshy surroundings away from main trading routes. Its inhabitants were occupied in the usual basic trades such as bakery, tailoring and weaving and they lived off small-scale agriculture, cattle farming and fishing. By 1648 the number of houses was reduced to 79 and the population had declined to 800 as a result of fires, the plague and the devastation of the Thirty Years War. Apart from this, in the course of history the overlord had rented off the castle and town no less than eighteen times to members of the Brandenburg aristocracy. The situation changed when Elector Frederick William, known as the Great Elector from 1675 onwards, developed an interest in the area mainly because of the excellent hunting prospects. He bought back the surrounding villages and finally the town of Potsdam, uniting them under his power. The old castle which Electress Katharina had modified in Renaissance style at the end of the 16. century was replaced by a new palace built in Dutch style. It was erected between 1662 and 1669 to designs by Johann Gregor Memhardt (about 1615 – about 1678). The Elector's years of study

Entrance to Potsdam Town Palace.
Etching by Pieter Schenk, 1702

in the Netherlands and his marriage to Luise Henriette, Princess of Orange, formed close connections to the most progressive European country of the time. Dutch artisans immigrated and model farms were set up but the most noticeable areas of Dutch influence were painting, sculpture, architecture and landscape gardening.

Numerous smaller buildings were erected in the vicinity of the palace and were interconnected by tree-lined avenues or waterways. The overall impression was reminiscent of Cleves on the Lower Rhine where Johann Moritz, a governor under the Great Elector, first realized his comprehensive landscape concepts. He also made suggestions for Potsdam and was probably responsible for the actual designs. The idea of a grand cultural landscape lived on throughout the following centuries but did

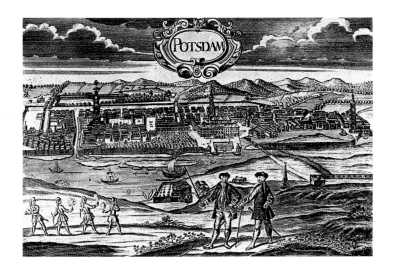

View of Potsdam from the Brauhausberg.
Copperplate engraving by Christian Friedrich Feldmann, about 1735

not reach its final shape until two hundred years later when Peter Joseph Lenné added his impressive contribution.

Under the Great Elector Potsdam had become the second residence of the Hohenzollern next to Berlin and it remained so until the fall of the monarchy in 1918. Every year the Great Elector spent much of his time at Potsdam from 1671 onwards. As a result of this he extended the palace in the direction of the Old Market between 1679 and 1682. Here he signed the famous "Edict of Potsdam" in 1685 which allowed Hugenots expelled from France to settle in Brandenburg-Prussia. In so doing he promoted economic growth and artistic creativity as well as the idea of tolerance. This subsequently became a maxim of Prussian politics and furthered the influence of various approaches and styles in Potsdam's architecture. The town itself grew during the Great

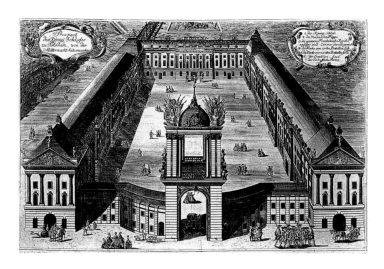

Bird's eye view of the Town Palace and Fortuna Portal.
Copperplate engraving by Johann David Schleuen the elder, after 1755

Elector's lifetime, mainly towards the west; plans to extend it towards the north remained impracticable as land conditions there were still far too swampy. Frederick III, the Great Elector's son, also took a great interest in Potsdam. Unlike his father, he looked more towards France for inspiration. To mark his coronation as first King of Prussia at Königsberg in 1701 he appointed Jean de Bodt, a Hugenot, to erect the Fortuna Portal at the entrance to the Town Palace. Schlüter contributed to the interior decoration of the palace which became a focal point for luxurious court occasions such as the Epiphany Meeting in 1709. Things changed, however, after Frederick William I, the "Soldier King", came to power in 1713. The emphasis in architectural activity was shifted away from the palace and into the town which by 1740 had grown so large that "it should no longer be

View of Sanssouci summer residence and gardens.
Etching by Johann Friedrich Schleuen the younger, after 1755

seen as a small town but ranked among the major towns" (Nicolai). In 1713 there were 199 houses in Potsdam and 1500 inhabitants; by 1740 there were 1154 houses and a population of 11,708. This rapid growth was caused by the transfer of various regiments from a number of towns in Brandenburg who were then accommodated in civilian quarters. During this period streets in the old part of the town were straightened and new houses were built, extending the town twice to the north in 1722 and 1733. Potsdam was now characterized by a system of straight roads and rectangular squares surrounded by uniform apartment houses of which the upper story was reserved for military personnel. The four blocks comprising the Dutch Quarter were characteristically designed for immigrants from the country for which particular attachment was still felt. Three new churches were built, con-

South-east side of Bassinplatz with the French Church.
Etching by Andreas Ludwig Krüger, 1779

trasting sharply with the simple lines of the domestic architecture and their spires, especially that of the Garrison Church, added recognizable highlights to the town's silhouette. A wall was built to prevent soldiers from deserting and help contain the smuggling of contraband goods. There were many town gates but the only one still remaining is the Hunter's Gate (Jägertor). As there were four thousand soldiers to be provided for Potsdam not only became a garrison town but also a manufacturing centre. The arrival of the military had changed both the character and the architectural image of the town. At that time comparisons were drawn between Sparta and Potsdam which after 1740, under Frederick the Great, was developed into an Athens. Whilst the military remained the architectural image of the town again began to change. The Town Palace was modified into a winter

Nikolai Church at the Old Market with Town Palace and Town Hall.
Watercolour by Ferdinand von Arnim, about 1850

residence by Knobelsdorff whilst a summer residence and park were created beyond the town's Brandenburg Gate at Sanssouci. By 1786 more than 600 of the simple domestic structures were replaced by representative town houses designed mainly by Georg Wenzeslaus v. Knobelsdorff (1699–1753), Carl v. Gontard (1731–1791) and Georg Christian Unger (1745–1799). Two or three buildings were often visually united beneath a single facade and – as in the day of the "Soldier King" – made over to the citizens of the town on the undertaking that the external appearance remain unaltered. This particular regulation ensured that the outer image of Potsdam remained virtually unchanged until the late 19. century. Frederick the Great not only made pre-liminary drawings for buildings and gardens at Sanssouci; he also designed houses for the town, specifying their size and location.

Similarly, his sketches of buildings in Italian, French and English style to be erected at specific points in the town also served as a guideline for the domestic architects. Such specialities in Potsdam still standing today include: the former Town Hall (after Palladio) at the Old Market (Alter Markt), the Hiller-Brandtsche-Houses in Wilhelm-Külz-Strasse (after Inigo Jones) and the gate, Nauener Tor, which was the first English influenced, neo-Gothic construction to be built on the continent. Classic lines in architecture can be seen in the Brandenburg Gate leading out to Sanssouci and in the Belvedere which stands on Klausberg. The gate, Neustädter Tor, which is no longer standing, represented a variation of Viennese baroque whilst eastern Asian elements are reflected in the Tea House (Teehaus) and the Dragon House (Drachenhaus). The plan to also build a mosque during the 19. century was never realized. Dutch elements were retained in the houses designed by Gontard and erected around the pool (Bassin).

Algarotti was right: Potsdam had already become a "school of architecture" and was to remain so for another hundred years. Apart from one small extension the town kept its basic shape. Along the arterial roads suburbs slowly developed but they did not gain in real significance until the 19. und 20. centuries. By the end of Frederick the Great's era the population had risen to 19,500, plus 9,000 military personnel – Potsdam was still "a school in the art of war".

Towards the end of the 18. century the town's importance dwindled as neighbouring Berlin rapidly grew. Building activity and the economy declined. Frederick's successor, his nephew Frederick William II, had a new garden (Neuer Garten) laid out and commissioned Gontard and Carl Gotthard Langhans (1737–1808) to build the Marmorpalais, a palace in early classicist style. The few new major buildings of this era included the Theatre which unfortunately is no longer standing, the Schauspielerkaserne and the Palais Lichtenau.

View of Glienicke Bridge seen from the Potsdam side of the Havel. Etching by Adrian Zingg after Sebastian Karl Christian Reinhardt, about 1795

Napoleon's defeat of Prussia in 1806, the French occupation which caused great suffering to the town and the ensuing Wars of Liberation also brought years of economic stagnation to Potsdam. It only recovered after several government agencies were transfered to the town; Potsdam was now not only a seat of residence and a military town but also a civil service centre. Building began again slowly after 1815. Karl Friedrich Schinkel set lasting architectural standards when he designed the palaces at Glienicke, Charlottenhof and Babelsberg as well as the particularly notable Nikolai Church which characterizes the town's silhouette to this day. Schinkel was Prussia's most famous architect during the first half of the 19. century; Peter Joseph Lenné (1789–1866) was his equally gifted counterpart in landscape design. He was active in Potsdam from 1816 until his death. A plan was developed for the "enhancement of the Isle of Potsdam", linking up with ideas from the late 17. century. The plan united the old and the new parks as well as the intermediary areas to form a vast "green" synthesis of the arts. It was Frederick William IV who inspired and promoted the project which included buildings in Italian, Norman and Oriental style by the Schinkel pupil Ludwig Persius (1805–1845), August Stüler (1800–1865), Ferdinand v. Arnim (1814–1866) and Luwig Ferdinand Hesse (1795–1876). Apart from this many villas were built and some time later, on the outskirts of the town, apartment houses and quarters for the troops. By the end of the 19. century Potsdam's population had risen to over 60,000. After the fall of the monarchy in 1918, the town ceased to be a royal seat of residence, though it continued to use this title. Even so, it managed to cultivate its high artistic standards and the Einstein Tower designed by Mendelsohn added an element of outstanding modern architecture to the town's century-old tradition.

On 14. April 1945, just a few days before the end of the war, British bombers devastated sections of Potsdam. Exactly two hundred years after the laying of the foundation stone at Sanssouci, 856 houses in the inner town were completely destroyed, 248 were partially destroyed and 3,301 were badly damaged. The town hall and the Nikolai Church were successfully restored, whereas the remains of the Town Palace, the Garrison Church, the Church of the Holy Ghost and many baroque town houses were finally demolished. The war caused lasting scars to the face of the town from which it will never recover.

Over the past few decades construction programmes often ignored the town's old tradition of absorbing European ideas and integrating them into a harmonious overall concept. Nevertheless, there are so many fine examples of architectural design from the past three centuries that Potsdam can still justifiably be seen as a "school of architecture".

Jägertor (Hunter's Gate), Potsdam's oldest remaining town gate, built 1773

Brandenburger Strasse, looking east towards
the catholic church of St. Peter and Paul, built 1867/70

Brandenburger Strasse, looking west towards the Brandenburg Gate, built 1770

Restored ornate portal in the Dutch Quarter, Friedrich-Ebert-Strasse 28

Gabled houses in the Dutch Quarter, Mittelstrasse 39–43, built 1737

The Old Market with Town Hall (1753/55) and Knobelsdorff House (1750),
Obelisk (1753/55) and Nikolai Church (1830/49)

Knobelsdorff House at the Old Market;
facade and balcony figures by F.Chr. Glume

The French Church on Bassinplatz, built 1751/53,
with sculptures by F.Chr. Glume

*Entrance to the former Royal Stables, now a film museum,
built 1685/1746, sculptures by F.Chr. Glume*

*Nauener Gate, built 1755 by J.G. Büring after a sketch
by Frederick the Great, modified 1867/68*

Uniform structures in Dutch style "Am Bassin", built 1773/85
by C. v. Gontard

*Intersection of Dortu-Strasse and Wilhelm-Külz-Strasse with a wing
of the former Military Orphanage, built 1771/72 by C. v. Gontard*

*Wilhelm-Külz-Strasse 9–12, the so-called Hiller-Brandtsche Houses
erected 1769 by G. Chr. Unger after an English design*

Two-storey late baroque residential houses in Kiezstrasse,
built 1777/80 by G.Chr. Unger

Wilhelm-Staab-Strasse, built 1777/85 by Gontard, Unger and Krüger;
restored 1955/56

*House at the corner of Schwertfegerstrasse and Friedrich-Ebert-Strasse,
one of the "Eight Corners", built by Gontard 1771*

*Burgstrasse 32/33, the Priest House belonging
to the Heiligengeist Church, built 1781 by G.Chr. Unger*

*Facade of the Langer Stall, former equestrian exercise hall,
built 1781 by G.Chr. Unger*

Wilhelm-Külz-Strasse 13, former Corporation House,
now Potsdam Museum, built 1770 by G.Chr. Unger

Posthofstrasse 17, former Schauspieler-Kaserne,
built 1796 by Boumann the younger; relief design by J.G. Schadow

Behlertstrasse 31, Palais Lichtenau, built 1796 by
Boumann the younger assisted by C.G. Langhans

*Mangerstrasse 23/26, citadel-style apartment house,
built 1892 by E. Petzold*

Behlertstrasse 32, former bridge tennant's house, built 1792 by A. L. Krüger, modified 1853 into a towered villa by L. F. Hesse

Russian Orthodox church of Holy Alexander Newski,
built 1826/29 to plans by W. P. Stasow, assisted by K. F. Schinkel

House in the Russian Colony "Alexandrowka",
built 1827 in Russian log cabin style

The Jewish Cemetery on Pfingstberg, founded in 1743,
includes many gravestones from the 18. to 20. century

Belvedere on Pfingstberg, built by Stüler and Hesse,
1849/52 and 1860/62 after a sketch by Frederick William IV

*Heilandskirche, church at the port in Sakrow near Potsdam,
built 1841/43 to sketches by Frederick William IV and plans by Persius*

Church in Bornstedt, built 1855/56, extended 1882.
The cemetery includes graves of famous Potsdam architects and gardeners

The vinyard, established 1744, and Sanssouci Palace, built 1745/47

*Circle around the Grand Fountain with marble figures
by the French sculptors L. S. and F. G. Adam, after 1750*

Chinese Tea House in Sanssouci park, built 1754/57 by J.G. Büring

The New Chambers to the west of Sanssouci Palace, built 1747
as an orangery by Knobelsdorff, converted into a guest house in 1770/72

*View from the roof of the New Palais towards
the belvedere on Klausberg, built 1770*

The New Palais in Sanssouci park, built 1763/69
by H. L. Manger, J. G. Büring and C. v. Gontard

Charlottenhof Palace, built 1826/29 by K. F. Schinkel
for Crown Prince Frederick William (IV)

View of the Roman Baths in Charlottenhof park, built 1829/35

The Orangery in Sanssouci park, with its Raphael Room,
historic chambers and viewing tower, built 1850/64

Triumphal Gate on Winzerberg, built 1851 after an ancient model in Rome

Steam engine house for the fountains at Sanssouci,
built 1841/42 in the form of a mosque

Sanssouci Gate at the entrance to the wildlife park,
built 1841/42 by L. Persius in the style of a medieval castle

Cecilienhof palace in the New Garden,
built 1912/16 by P. Schultze-Naumburg

*View across lake Heiligen See towards the Marmorpalais,
kitchen and pyramid in the New Garden*

*Entrance to Lindstedt palace, built 1857/61 as a retreat
for the aging Frederick William IV by L. F. Hesse*

*Babelsberg Castle, built 1834/49 in neo-Gothic style
for William I by Schinkel, Persius and Strack*

Glienicke Bridge, built 1907, connects Berlin and Potsdam

Einstein Tower, built 1920/21 by E. Mendelsohn
for research on the relativity theory

Useful Information

Potsdam-Information Centre

Friedrich-Ebert-Straße 5
1560 Potsdam
Tel.: 21 100
Fax: 23 012
Mon–Fri 9am–8pm
Sat/Sun 9am–6pm

Happy Car

Travel Service and car rent
Hotel Schloss Cecilienhof
Neuer Garten
1561 Potsdam
Tel.: 22 842

Museums

Sanssouci Palace

Tel.: 23 931
Guided tours daily
Closed every 1. & 3. Monday
of the month

New Palais

Tel.: 93 143
Guided tours daily
Closed every 2. & 4. Monday
of the month
Open as museum to the general
public during summer months

New Chambers

Tel.: 22 823
Guided tours daily
Closed Fridays

"The Mosque" Steam Engine House

Tel.: 24 106
Open Sat/Sun (winter) and
Wed–Sun (summer) 9am–4pm

Ladies Wing of Sanssouci Palace*

Tel.: 23 931

Picture Gallery*

Tel.: 22 655

Orangery*

with viewing tower
Tel.: 26 189

Chinese Tea House*

Tel.: 93 628

Charlottenhof Palace*

Tel.: 92 774

Roman Baths*

Tel.: 93 211

"Stern" Hunting Lodge*

Tel.: 62 12 44
Open Sat/Sun only

Bookings for guided tours
of the above historic buildings
and museums:
Visitors Information
(Besucherbetreuung)
Am Grünen Gitter 2
Potsdam Sanssouci
Tel.: 23 819

* Only open for viewing
during summer months

Potsdam Film Museum

Am Karl-Liebknecht-Forum 1
1560 Potsdam
Tel.: 23 675
Open Tues–Sun 10am–5pm
Closed Mondays

Potsdam Museum

Wilhelm-Külz-Strasse 13
(former Corporation House)
History of Potsdam from
993 to 1900; nature and
environment around the Havel;
aquarium with fish of the Havel

Wilhelm-Külz-Str. 8–12
(Hiller-Brandtsche Houses)
History of Potsdam 1900–1945
Special exhibitions

Hegelallee 38
Karl Liebknecht Memorial
Museum
Visits and guided tours
by appointment.

Tel.: History/Memorial 23 182
Nature/Environment   23 782
Open Tues–Sun 10am–5pm

Memorial of the Potsdam Agreement at Cecilienhof

In the New Garden
Tel.: 22 579
Guided tours daily except
Monday 9am–4.15pm
Closed every 2. & 4. Monday
of the month

Botanical Garden

of Brandenburg Highschool
Maulbeerallee 2
Tel.: 91 05 76
Greenhouses open daily
9.30am–4pm; closed 12.30–1pm
Outdoor area closed to public

Galleries

Gallery "Am Alten Markt",
Gallery "Blick",
Gallery "Im Turm"
all in Hans Marchwitza
Kulturhaus,
Am Alten Markt
Open Tues–Sun 10am–6pm

"potsdam galerie"

Am Staudenhof
(Am Alten Markt)
Tel.: 21 373
Open Tues–Sun 9am–5pm

Gallery "Samtleben"

Brandenburger Strasse 66
Tel.: 24 075

Gallery "TRAPEZ"
Wilhelm-Pieck-Strasse 27
Open Thurs–Sat 2–7pm

Erste unabhängige Kunstfabrik
(First independent Art Factory)
Hermann-Elflein-Strasse 10
Fri–Sun 11am–5pm

Jewish Cemetery
Puschkinallee 25,
Am Pfingstberg
Guided tours every 3. Sunday in
the month at 10am

Theatres
Hans-Otto-Theater Potsdam
Zimmerstrasse 10
Tel.: 46 51

Advance bookings at
Potsdam Information Centre
and 9 days in advance at the
theatre office,
Brandenburger Str. 18
Tel.: 23 038/23 190
Tues   11am–1pm; 2pm–5pm
Thurs 11am–1pm; 2pm–7pm
Fri/Sat 9am–1pm

Kleines Theater am Alten Markt
(In Hans Marchwitza Kulturhaus)

Potsdamer Kabarett am Obelisk
Schopenhauer-Strasse 27
Tel.: 21 069/21 738

Hotels
Hotel am Jägertor
Hegelallee 11, Tel.: 21 834/21 038

Hotel Schwielowsee
Strasse am Schwielowsee 110
Tel.: Werder 28 50

Hotel Babelsberg
Stahnsdorfer Str. 68
Tel.: 78 889

Hotel Bayrisches Haus
Wildpark, Tel.: 93 192/92 329

Hotel Hakelburg
Ph.-Müller-Allee 185
Kleinmachnow, Tel.: 22 858

Hotel Potsdam
Lange Brücke, Tel.: 46 31

Hotel Restaurant "Havelblick"
Frau Stöckigt, Tel.: 02 592/2 14
1501 Töplitz, Dorfstr. 17

Hotel Schloss Cecilienhof
Im Neuen Garten, Tel.: 23 141

Guest House
"Am Park Babelsberg"
An der Sternwarte 2,
Tel.: 76 23 31

Lindenpension

Frau Fischer, Kopernikusstr. 39
Tel.: 75 283

Touristen und Congresshotel

Otto-Grotewohl-Strasse 60
Tel.: 8 60

Private accommodation and bungalows bookable through Potsdam Information Centre

Friedrich-Ebert-Strasse 5
Tel.: 23 385

Markets

Weekly Market

Am Bassin
daily

Flea-Market

Babelsberg, Weberplatz
Sat 8am–4pm

Havelländer Grocery Market

B(L)AUHAUS open zone
Sat 8am–15pm

Grand Art and Flea-Market

B(L)AUHAUS open zone
Sun 9am–4pm

Boat Trips

Weisse Flotte Potsdam

Lange Brücke
Tel.: 42 41/ext. 2 47; Fax: 21 090
Info and Booking office:
Mon–Fri 8am–4pm

Bus Information Service

Tel.: 22 966

THE AUTHORS

MANFRED HAMM,
born 1944 in Zwickau, lives and works in Berlin as a photographer for German and overseas journals and art publishers. He was twice awarded the Kodak Photo-Book prize for: Berlin – Industrial Monuments (1978) and Coffee Houses (1979). Other works include: Railway Stations (1984); Berlin – Natural landscapes; Parks and Gardens (1985); Redbrick Buildings between Lübeck and Stralsund (1990) and Palaces and Gardens in Potsdam (1990)
– all published by Nicolai

HANS–JOACHIM GIERSBERG,
Dr. phil., born 1938, studied art history, history and ethnology at the Humboldt University, Berlin. Since 1964 research specialist for sculpture and since 1969 for the preservation of monuments at the State Palaces and Gardens, Potsdam-Sanssouci; appointed Director of the Palaces in 1978. Numerous publications on the art and cultural history of Potsdam, including: Potsdamer Veduten (1980), Potsdamer Schlösser in Geschichte und Kunst (1984), Friedrich als Bauherr (1986). He has also prepared exhibitions at home and abroad including: Karl-Friedrich Schinkel (Berlin 1980/81; Hamburg 1982/83), Friedrich II und die Kunst (Potsdam-Sanssouci 1986), Der Grosse Kurfürst (Potsdam-Sanssouci 1988)